FRESH EYES

FRESH EYES

I am creating something new.
There it is! Do you see it?
Isaiah 43:19

MIRANDA SMALLS

XULON PRESS

Xulon Press
2301 Lucien Way #415
Maitland, FL 32751
407.339.4217
www.xulonpress.com

Unless otherwise indicated, Scripture quotations taken from the Contemporary English
Version (CEV). Copyright © 1995 American Bible Society. Used by permission. All
rights reserved.

Scripture quotations taken from The Message (MSG). Copyright © 1993, 1994, 1995,
1996, 2000, 2001, 2002. Used by permission of NavPress Publishing Group. Used
by permission. All rights reserved.

Scripture quotations taken from the Holy Bible, New International Version (NIV).
Copyright © 1973, 1978, 1984, 2011 by Biblica, Inc.™. Used by permission. All rights
reserved.

Scripture quotations taken from the King James Version (KJV) – public domain.

Scripture quotations taken from the New American Standard Bible (NASB). Copyright
© 1960, 1962, 1963, 1968, 1971, 1972, 1973, 1975, 1977, 1995 by The Lockman
Foundation. Used by permission. All rights reserved.

Printed in the United States of America.

ISBN-13: 978-1-6628-0059-7

DEDICATION

This book is dedicated to my mother, Dorothy, in gratitude for my godly upbringing. Her prayers, love, and belief in me have sustained me. To the memory and legacy of my grandmother who instilled in me a love for God, reading, and a thirst for education; and to my daughter, Stephanie, and my grandsons, Jaylen and Nathaniel, for their motivation and encouragement.

TABLE OF CONTENTS

ACKNOWLEDGMENTS

Although my name appears on the cover of this book, I owe much gratitude to those people who contributed to the finished product. I must first acknowledge Jesus Christ my Lord and Savior. He is the ultimate source of my strength, the Alpha and Omega of my life, and the center of my joy. Without Him, none of this would have been possible.

To my Sister friend, Dorette, thank you for supporting me throughout this endeavor. You have helped me to polish this manuscript for which I am so grateful. You have been my prayer warrior, my editor, and my encourager.

Thanks to Pastor Elisa and Vivienne, two authors who supported me, prayed for me, and gave me advice.

I acknowledge my church—Rev. Dr. Marvin J. Bentley and my Antioch Baptist Church family. Thank you for your many prayers and well wishes.

I thank ALL my friends, but in particular, Richard, Marcel, Nisha, Altamease, Deacon Stevenson, and Rev. Bello. Thank you for the much-needed pep talks, lunches, and dinners that gave me a break from the writing process and for your consistent prayers and encouragement.

I truly thank my entire family for their prayerful support and assistance in so many areas. Thank you to my cousin, Naomi, who is the youngest author in our family. May you continue to inspire readers with your wonderful imagination as you author books for children.

Finally, I wish to thank the team at Xulon Press. Thank you for providing guidance and direction in what has been a long but exciting journey.

I am so thankful because I have been amazingly fortunate to have all of you in my life. To God be the glory, great things He has done!

ABOUT THE AUTHOR

Miranda Smalls is passionate about God, family, and education. She is keen on infusing the wisdom and knowledge that comes from the Scriptures in those around her. A native of Queens, New York, Miranda earned a bachelor's degree in Business Administration, and a master's degree in Educational Leadership from Baruch College. As she studied, she challenged herself to lead and educate those around her as well. Miranda served as Director of Christian Education in her church for more than 20 years, and has been teaching Sunday school for twice as long. Her zest for knowledge led her to successfully earn a doctoral degree in education from Concordia University in Chicago, Illinois.

Miranda's love for people, especially young people, charted her career path early on. After a brief stint in the public and private sectors, she worked for several years as a high school teacher and college advisor, and currently serves as an adjunct professor of English at a local college.

Miranda has conducted youth and leadership workshops for American Baptist Churches-Metro New York, and has designed several Sunday school workshops for churches around New York City. She has also served as a consultant for the American Bible Society, writing for their *Elementz of Life* youth magazine.

Fresh Eyes, her first book of poetry and reflections, has been a labor of love and is a testimony of her faith.

Introduction

Over and over the Scriptures tell us that we need to be transformed. In fact, when we accept Jesus Christ, the Bible says that old things pass away and new things come into focus (2 Corinthians 5:17). The Apostle Paul encourages us to renew our mind so that we can embrace those spiritual truths that God wants to reveal to us. As Christians, we walk by faith and not by sight. That means we don't have to wait for God to prove himself by showing us a miracle, because we know that he can, and he will, even before it manifests. We believe without seeing because "believing is seeing" since we now have "fresh eyes."

This book, *Fresh Eyes*, was born from whisperings from God to my heart, responses to trials, and observations of the world we live in. As an educator by profession, my heart longs for people to come to a knowledge of the Lord Jesus Christ. I rejoice when young people take hold of education and let it propel them to the next level. I am thrilled when each of us holds the rope for the other to climb up, and for all of us to respond in gratitude.

Life is no bed of roses. If it were, then we all would be horticulturists. Daily we fight trials and temptations. We struggle to be "in" the world, but not be "of" the world. We persevere only by the grace of God and the wisdom he applies to our hearts.

The writer of the Book of James tells us to ask God for wisdom, and God will give it to us in generous fashion (James 1:5). I believe that, and so it is my hope that you will find nuggets of wisdom in the pages of this book and the Scripture references that are listed. I pray, that as you read, you will be blessed; that you will find something that makes you laugh, causes you to scratch your head, or makes you reach for your Bible.

I appreciate your taking the time to read this. So, walk by faith, not by sight with *Fresh Eyes*!

Section I

Bullying: My Story

...Don't try to get even. Let God take revenge.
Romans 12:19

I was raised in a wonderful, urban community where I was surrounded by great neighbors, fun-filled street activities, annual block parties, and everyone on the block treated each other like family. The downside was that some kids did not respect my space nor did they respect me. They teased me, picked on me, and tormented me. Growing up, I was bullied.

I was an average 10-year-old student in the fifth grade. I had to study hard to get good grades unlike my peers who seemed to just glide through school easily. My mother was deeply vested in my education, but as a single parent, she also had to work at nights to make ends meet. I can recall many mornings that my grandmother prepared pancakes and bacon or sausage, eggs and grits (and yes, it was good!) for me in my Mom's absence.

Although my grandmother only had a fifth grade education, her heart's desire was that her children and grandchildren embrace education. She would always tell me, "I send you to school to learn, not to fight." Every morning I left the house with my grandmother's words ringing in my ears because I knew grandma did not play. She meant every word she said.

My stomach tightened and my palms began to sweat each time I left home. I would tell myself, "Self, calm down. Maybe today they won't be there." But they were. They always were.

There were two of them—a tall, thin girl and her short, hefty sidekick. The female Batman and Robin? No! They were not my Caped Crusaders since these two made it their business to hurt me, not help me. Their one and only job every morning was to torment me and several other kids.

Every morning, about two blocks from my house, they would wait for me. Although I would try to go a different way, it wasn't long before they found my new route. They would take my lunch (because back then I didn't carry money) and I just let them have it. They would tease me and call me names and although it hurt me badly, I just would silently cringe inside. The two would take turns pushing me, egged on perhaps by the fact that I didn't say a word. I endured this torture for about a month before I finally told my mother and grandmother. To boost my confidence, they began to take turns walking me to school. Thank God, the bullying subsided.

My young mind could not understand such mean-spiritedness. Why are they doing this? I wondered, as I cried myself to sleep night after night. I am a good person, I thought. I attend church every Sunday. I am in Sunday school. I read my Bible. I sing in the choir. I am not someone who cut school or has a behavior problem, or sass the teachers. So why is this happening to me?

My grandmother stopped walking me to school because the torment had let up considerably. But one day, in the supermarket across the street from my house, as I was alone shopping for my family, I saw them. The bully duo was in the store! They viciously slammed their cart into mine. I tried to ignore them because I knew I could not stand up against two of them. I was deathly afraid and they knew that. I just stayed in one of the aisles until I thought they were gone.

As the grocery clerk packed my groceries, I held my breath, desperately praying that they wouldn't be outside. My heart almost stopped beating. They were waiting for me. I could not escape their menacing looks and taunting gestures. With two bags of groceries, one in each arm, I proceeded out the door. Door. They started pushing me and teasing me over and over until I got in front of my house. **I HAD ENOUGH!** I jumped on the tall, slim girl and grabbed her by her hair and knocked her to the sidewalk. I began to ram her head into the sidewalk until I heard my grandmother scream as she ran out the house. "Don't kill her!" When they pulled me off her, she got up, put her tail between her legs and ran. Her sidekick, the one who often provoked the taunting, was long gone before the fight began.

I didn't feel great about getting into a fight, but I was tired. Tired of being picked on. Tired of being pushed. Tired of being afraid. Most of all tired of these two girls interrupting my education and tired of having no control over my life. **I JUST HAD ENOUGH!**

As I grew older, I prayed that I would have the opportunity to protect children so that none of them would have to experience the torment I went through. God gave me that opportunity. I became a teacher and a licensed guidance counselor. I've had to walk students home because other students wanted to jump them. I've had to stop a fight in a store's parking lot where five girls were planning to jump one girl. It's ingrained in me not to let this happen to anyone else even at the risk of my own safety. Crazy, huh?

So what would you do if you were being bullied? Chances are you would be scared for your safety. Chances are you would try to deflect the issue by being compliant and allowing them, without a fuss, to take your possessions as I did. Or you'd practice avoidance by hiding away from school or the neighborhood hangouts. But you'll learn that bullies thrive on your cowardice, and the more fearful you are of them, the more pleasure they get out of the attack and the more they step up the pressure. So what can you do besides fight or flight?

I can tell you from experience that you must tell someone—a school faculty member or administrator, a parent, family member, pastor or a friend. Don't keep it bottled up inside of you like I did, but pray that the person you tell will listen to you, not only with their ears, but also with their heart. Here's some radical advice—pray for the bully. The Bible tells us to pray for our enemies, for those who spitefully abuse and misuse us. Is it easy? Not by a long shot, but it does work. Read and study God's Word. One of my favorite Bible verses is, *"When you pass through the waters, I will be with you; And through the rivers, they will not overflow you. When you walk through the fire, you will not be scorched, Nor will the flame burn you"* (Isaiah 43:2, NASB). God has given us his Word that he will be there for us. I had my trial by fire and I know now that I did not solve it in the right way because I could have been seriously hurt or I could have severely injured the bully.

Bullying often scars its victims physically and psychologically. It traumatizes them so that they become stressed and depressed and may eventually avoid going to classes, extracurricular sports, and other activities. Bullying in any form should not be tolerated. Parents and teachers need to teach young people, from an early age, the concept of tolerance. We must show by our words and our actions that we accept and embrace diversity in others. It is a concept to which I wholeheartedly subscribe.

Basic Training

*Dear friends, you must never
become tired of doing right.*
2 Thessalonians 3:13

5:00 a.m.
Basic Training begins.
You in?
Yeah, I'm in.

Well, take a big dose of respect every morning
Coupled with some morning prayer,
Then take some supplements of "Please" and
"Thank You"
And use as needed here and there.

When necessary say, "I'm sorry"
To soothe your mind and soul,
Remember, you're not always right.
Forgive and let go of the load.

Speak when you enter a room,
That's why people continue to stare
Because they were holding a conversation
Before you made an appearance there.

Wash your hands before you eat,
Don't be so quick to hungrily partake
Of the food God gives—first, thank the Giver
And bless your food for goodness sake.

12:00 Noon
You still with me?
Basic Training isn't quite over
It's about to take a turn
To assess what you have learned.
Are you still in?
I'm in.

Respect for your elders.
Basic Training
Give up your seat to the elderly.
Basic Training
Hold the door for the person behind you.
Basic Training

Let a pregnant woman sit down.
Basic Training
No singing at the table
Basic Training
A child in grown folks' business – Oh, no!
Basic Training.

You in?
I'm in.
These little things separate
The polished from the crass.
Basic Training
End of class.

A Young Person's Cry

Rescue the perishing; don't hesitate to step in and help. Proverbs 24:11, MSG

If you want to know me
Yeah, I'm different from the others.
But for many years you've heard
Don't judge a book by its cover.

I have many *"body"* covers
It's difficult to show my feelings,
I hide behind a mask
'cause I need some inner healing.

Can I talk to you?
Will you go deeper than the surface?
Will you be my spiritual lifeguard
And show me that GOD has a purpose?

Will you motivate and encourage me
Despite my "outside" clothes,
Or will you think of an excuse
Because I'm too much of a load?

Will you take the time to mold me
In your simple, human way
By pointing me to the Great Potter
Who can reshape my broken clay?

Will you be my spiritual lifeguard
Even though we didn't grow up the same?
Will you look deeper than the surface
To see I'm more than just a name?

I'm scared, so very scared
To present myself as a "living sacrifice."
Deep inside I want it so bad
But keep taking the wrong advice.

To all of my mentors—family, friends, and leaders,
I want to change, please don't give up on me.
Keep letting God use you as my lifeguard
Because **I'M MORE THAN
WHAT YOU SEE!**

Quit Messin' with your Dreams

The LORD God appeared to him in a dream...
Please make me wise and teach me the
difference between right and wrong.
1 Kings 3:5, 9a

Every day I sit here and wonder how you make it
When you're smart enough to do it
But continually fake it.
Fake what?
That you're not
Smart enough
Good enough
Tough enough
To survive.
My goodness, you live for a grade of 65!
But don't sit here like you don't know what I mean,
I'm trying to understand why
You keep messin' with your dreams.

Don't go to class—then ask for the pass,
Then you wonder how long the class is gonna last.
Have no problem textin'
In the middle of a lesson.
Hand in half of the work
Then wonder why the grade you get is less than dirt!
Dirt, Yeah I said, Dirt.
You can rise,
Reach for the skies,
Stop telling those lies
To yourself.
Maybe it's me and all this is not what it seems
But somehow I believe that
You're still messin' with your dreams.

Young ladies, you are queens!
Young men, you are kings!
You have to understand your purpose
So that you can accomplish many things.
Many things, like what?
Not just sitting in class
But gaining knowledge,
Preparing for your future...
Prepare to go to college.

But please, no more excuses. Please don't let
me scream.
Am I wrong or am I right?
Are you still messin' with your dreams?

If you know the Lord,
Praise his name!
(And don't be ashamed.)
If you do well in school,
Don't be a fool
And break the rules
(Just to be cool).
If you have a talent
Don't let it get to your head
Stay blessed and humble
(And share your gift instead).
Too many died so that all of you could live
And you sit here and tell me that you don't
want to give...
Give what?

Give back to those who paved the way
So you could sit
Where you want on public transportation,

Or be taught in a school and get a proper education.
Can you show the world that they didn't die in vain?
Can't you hear their wounded hearts
Crying out to you in pain?
You're better than that!
You're stronger than that!
You're more talented than that!
You're more beautiful than that!
You're more intelligent than that!
You have more integrity than that!

If you're good, stay good.
If you're not, step up.
Life is too short, and sometimes it's not what it seems.
You have no time to waste,
So quit messin' with your dreams!

Let Me Apologize

Teach your children right from wrong...
Proverbs 22:6

Please let me apologize for my actions the other day. I never thought it was impolite for a teacher to care about her students, regardless of color, race, religion, or gender, perhaps more than they care about themselves...

Please excuse my manners when I try to cut the umbilical cord of laziness and disrespect that some try to hold on to for dear life. I just try to challenge what I know is deep inside each of you.

Oh yes! Did I forget to apologize to those who complain about writing a paragraph, an essay, a paper, not to mention reading for at least 30 minutes a day? Please let me apologize on behalf of all the ancestors who died and didn't have the opportunity to learn to read or write. They would have loved to be taught, to sit in your seat.

And, oh my goodness, how thoughtless of me not to apologize to those who are asked to pick up a pen and pencil, bring a notebook to school, and do a little more work other than complain constantly. Let me apologize for mentioning that maybe you should turn off the television and the video games sometimes so your work won't suffer...

Wow! I forgot to apologize for being grateful that my students can take another breath and see another day filled with vision and expectation. I need to apologize to you, young men, for teaching you to respect me by pulling up your pants. And to you, young women, for asking you to dress appropriately. Let me just continue to apologize for reminding you to watch how you speak to others, and about others. Or to be aware that social media can be a powerful tool to lift people up or tear people down.

Let me apologize to you for caring enough to share this. Truly, I apologize...

Mentor

Tell the young men to have self-control in everything. Always set a good example for others. Be sincere and serious when you teach. Titus 2:6-7

To Uncle Pete, everyone's story was important and everyone's opinion was valued. He had an innate ability to understand others and a fierce determination to inspire and help as many people as he could. As the owner of the corner grocery store, Uncle Pete gave me my first job (volunteer) bagging groceries at 10 years old. It was in this corner grocery store that I witnessed the power of mentoring at work.

Day in, day out, young men would come into the store to talk to Uncle Pete. Some came for basic advice, but many of them, who had been beaten and broken by the streets of life, came for words of encouragement and support which they so seldom received from the adults in their lives. Uncle Pete gave them liberally; never looking at them with judgmental or condescending eyes, but listening to them with his ears, his eyes, and his heart as he uplifted them far above the narrow world in which they lived.

I often reflect on those days in the grocery store and the hundreds of people Uncle Pete helped, but I was particularly amazed at the large numbers of young boys who came into his store day and night. He not only gave them jobs, where possible, or sage fatherly advice, but he truly showed that he cared and the young men he mentored responded to it.

Roosevelt "Pete" Woodard's nurture of the young men in our community opened my eyes. I realized that I, too, wanted to make a difference in the lives of youth, and for years I have been especially concerned about our young men. From Gloria Steinem's, *"Take Your Daughter to Work Day"* (which has since been changed to include sons) to witnessing in my own classroom how boys learn differently from girls, to viewing the documentary *"Raising Cain,"* I began to wonder the extent to which other young men would have been able to achieve their dreams if they had an *"Uncle Pete"* in their lives who cared about them unconditionally and who would push them to achieve their greatest potential. It was, indeed, this social and intellectual curiosity that put me in pursuit of finding answers.

This essay is adapted from the Introduction to my Doctoral Dissertation on Mentoring. It was originally titled, "From School Boys to Successful Men: What Factors Contribute to an Effective Mentoring Relationship for African-American Males?"

I'M A SUCCESS STORY

*I will bless you with a future filled with
hope—a future of success...* Jeremiah 29:11

You only see the outside
Never my talent, my soul, or my purpose.
You only judge me by my mistakes
But never look at who I really am.
Who am I?
I'm a Success Story.

Made some mistakes in my life.
Had to pick up a whole lot of pieces,
Learned from broken dreams,
Built my spirit brick by brick and piece by piece
Until one day I realized
I'm a Success Story.

Tried to understand why my daddy left me,
Couldn't understand why mama
Struggled to keep me.
It was so hard to be all I needed to be
When every message was,

"You'll be nothing more than a failure."
But look at me now.
I'm a Success Story.

They talked about me and scandalized my name.
They tried to shake down my character
And my integrity.
They tried to use me, confuse me, and abuse me
But some vases are hard to break.
Say what you want
I'm a Success Story.

I didn't realize that I could soar above the clouds,
I didn't realize that I could touch the sky.
It took some time for me to untangle some issues
And break down the walls of unforgiveness and pain,
But don't let the outside shell fool you because
I'm a Success Story.

Not a failure
Not a dirty shame
Not an unspoken secret
Not a black sheep
Not a lost cause

Because I have a Beautiful Mind
A Resilient Spirit
I'm a Dream Maker
A Goal Seeker
A Risk Taker
An Independent Thinker
A Family Man
A Woman of Worth
An Agent of Change
I have a Prosperous Future
A College-Bound Future
A Career-Oriented Future

I'm more powerful than I even imagined.
God put me here for a purpose and
"I'm More Than a Conqueror"
I'm a S-U-C-C-E-S-S
And mirrors don't tell lies—
I'm a Success Story.

Section II

LET THE RAINBOW REMIND US

The rainbow that I have put in the sky will be
my sign to you and to every living creature on
earth. It will remind you that I will keep this
promise forever. Genesis 9:12-13

Every time I get into
a tailspin about things
I think about a Rainbow
and the beauty that it brings.
Those brilliant colors
give me hope for tomorrow,
They challenge my hard times,
bitterness, or sorrow.

But what if this Rainbow
represents the beauty in you and me,
Would there be something deep inside
we wouldn't want others to see?
Do we promise to love God,
and our neighbor as ourselves,
Yet place that promise out of sight
on some high-reaching shelf?

Let the Rainbow remind us
 that we're made in varying hues,
Vanilla, Caramel, Chocolate,
 Pecan, Mocha, and Ebony, too.
 This skin that we've been born with
 sometimes saddles us with blame.
 But we walk worthy in God's blessings,
We will not hide our heads in shame.

If the Rainbow reminds us of anything,
It's that our God is very real.
He's a faithful promise keeper
who provides, protects, and heals.
There's a generation that's behind us
 evaluating our myths, truths and facts.
They want to know if the faith we profess
Is merely not an act.

We are as beautiful as God's Rainbow
which adorns the rain-drenched sky,
But beauty quickly fades away
once love begins to die.
So let the Rainbow remind us
to love each other and then agree

To leave to those who follow God's Word
A perfect legacy.

Precious Baby

Children are a blessing and a gift from the
Lord. Psalm 127:3

Oh this is wonderful day of celebration,
What a joy and what a pleasure.
You have been blessed to expand your family,
And make room for your new treasure.

A precious little newcomer
To have and to hold
With smiles that are more precious
Than silver and gold.

He'll demolish your schedule
'Though he's helpless and small,
He'll make his needs known
And he'll rule over all.

You will see as he gets older
Sometimes your work can't be done
Because the "miracle baby" will say,
"It's my time to have fun."

When you hear him start laughing
You'll keep "aahing" and "oohing,"
And he'll keep on replying
By "gaga" and "gooing"

But as he grows older
He'll look to you with innocent eyes,
And expect you to give him
Advice that is wise.

To make sense of it all
He'll look to his parents first.
And you should remind him
That he was a *"miracle"* birth.

Remind him that he was
In God's plan from the start.
Then continually remind yourself
You have the leading role in his heart.

God has loaned this precious baby to you
So lead and direct your little boy,
The blessing you prayed for is now yours—
Your beautiful bundle of joy.

Some people may still have doubts
That God works miracles today,
But you and I have proven
That God answers when we pray.

Let's praise God for his blessings,
He gives us good things to enjoy,
You only have to look around at
Your precious baby boy.

ONLY CHILD

"...Do not forget your mother's teaching."
Proverbs 1:8, NIV

When I was just a little girl
You taught me how to pray.
I remember nights spent on our knees
Like it was yesterday.

You taught me how to fight life's battles
No matter how difficult they were.
I'll never forget when I was sick,
Your faith helped me to endure

You taught me how to be a lady
From the time I was a teen,
But even more than that
You taught me how to live, to laugh, to dream.

You gave me more than I could ask
With your silent strength and love.
You sacrificed your best for me and
God blessed you with his love.

Now when I pause and ponder,
And my thoughts sometimes run wild,
I always smile when I remember
I'll forever be your one and only child.

Two Words

The LORD is my God! I will praise him and tell him how thankful I am. Psalm 118:28

Can I talk to you for a moment?
And I caution you this may get a little deep
But we came here today for a purpose
Not to just occupy these seats.

You see, I just want to talk to you about two words
That so many take for granted.
I know you may have to dig deep in your mind
To see if they were ever planted.

Oh yeah, you know the two words
That so many people fail to use,
But let me take a moment to remind you
Just in case you are confused.

THANK YOU are the two words.
Gratitude will always win it!
It's not like you're giving the shirt off your back
This will only take a minute.

This tribute is to say "Thank you!"
To some unsung heroes today.
To those who unselfishly give of themselves
In so many different ways.

Thanks to the Essential Workers
For putting your lives on the line,
For being there for us and our loved ones
When we're living, and when we're dying.

Thank you for showing us courage
In the face of challenging tests,
For not giving up when hope seemed dim,
For giving of your very best.

We salute every branch of the military
And those who died defending our nation.
We thank you today for your sacrifice.
You've earned our utmost admiration.

If we take a good look within our hearts,
This tribute is long overdue.
Essential workers and military personnel
We neglected to say, "Thank you."

So when someone goes quite out of their way
To do a good deed or two,
Don't hesitate to acknowledge the debt,
And say a hearty, "Thank you!"

Just two words, and they are oh so small,
Yet they're used by only a few.
Please use them lavishly when you can:
You'll smile when they come back to you.

Where Do You Stand?

My dear friends, stand firm and don't be shaken... 1 Corinthians 15:58

You may stand on a big stage
Because you want to be seen.
Or you may stand in the middle
And be crushed in between.

You may stand in a shower
Because you want to be clean,
Or stand in someone's face
Because you feel like being mean.

You can stand for the Pledge of Allegiance
And the Star Spangled Banner, too.
But will you stand on the Word of God
And allow it to change you?

You can stand behind a podium
Because you want to be heard,
But in this time of crisis
We all need God's Holy Word.

How then will you stand
In a world that's vile and mean?
You focus your mind on God's promises
Like Philippians 4:13.

We can do ALL things through Christ
Because he makes us strong.
He calms our fears in the midst of a storm,
He gives us victory over wrong.

So when your way seems strange or dark,
Ask God to take your hand.
He will guide you to the one true light,
He'll teach you, by faith, to stand.

ALL YOU NEEDED
WAS THE WORD

I treasure your word above all else.
Psalm 119:11

Chances are you've been lied to.
There are people on your job who have tried you.
Thought you were going to Rikers, but you let the
Lord guide you
Because all you needed was the WORD...
    the WORD came through.

Chances are you have bills that are late.
You are sitting here with too much on your plate.
You don't see eye to eye, yes! you and your mate
But all you needed was the WORD...
    the WORD changed you.

Chances are you've been feelin' really down,
Stressin' 'bout things when no one was around.
It seems that your life has been turned upside down.
But all you needed was the WORD...
    the WORD made a way.

Chances are you still recall the many lies they told,
How lying, cheating, stealing
Would bring a pot of gold.
Perhaps it almost trapped you,
But you managed to be bold
Because all you needed was the WORD...
    the WORD told you what to say.

Many of my battles are being fought uphill,
But the Word of God tells me,
"Stand strong and be still!"
Thank you God for your Word,
I am trusting in your will.
All I needed was the WORD...
    the WORD saved me!

Section III

Forever Wonderful

Every time I think of you, I thank my God.
Philippians 1:3

Every time I picture each of you,
The scenes in my mind roll back
to beautiful memories.
Memories of laughter, hard work, love and creativity.
Memories of challenging, but fabulous times
touching lives,
So my prayer for each you is to stay
FOREVER WONDERFUL.

Every time I think of your resilient spirit,
Your dedicated, supportive, kind and blessed spirit,
I ask God to shower each of you with raindrops
of blessings.
May he embrace you with His Word
as you move forward.
So my prayer continues to be for you to stay
FOREVER WONDERFUL.

Every time I think of how you've touched a young
person's life,
How you have given of yourselves unconditionally,
How you have sacrificed your time...
My hope is that you balance your lives
and continue to shine
As you deepen your faith and stay
FOREVER WONDERFUL.

Every time I think of your awesome gifts
That only a mighty and majestic God can give,
I realize that an "Incredible God Deserves
Incredible Praise."
So I give God glory for what you've done,
And the greater things you will do, only He knows.
But for now, my heart and soul can just tell you
to always be
FOREVER WONDERFUL
To children, to youth, but most of all, to God!

WEAPONS OF MASS DISTRACTION

...I have become all things to all people so
that by all possible means I might save some.
1 Corinthians 9:22, NIV

I

Let's face it, ladies—like it or not—we are "weapons of mass distraction!" Do you hear those wolf whistles as we walk down the street? Do you see the construction worker almost losing his footing (and his mind) on the scaffolding as we pass by? It didn't start with us. Adam was left in charge, but in no time Eve had him eating out of her hand! (Here, baby! Good fruit! Eat this!). As the old saying goes, "Men can't live with us and they can't live without us."

But what's this about a weapon? Many men say that our most powerful weapons are in our upper body or our lower body—tight jeans, low-cut shirts, see-through blouses, high heeled shoes...need I go on? When we walk we can make heads turn, cars crash, and people whisper. Yet, we women also know that we have other weapons at our disposal. We may pull out weapons of anger, jealousy, and envy. These weapons are so powerful they can actually do real damage to someone. For centuries, men (and some women) have been trying to figure us out. The funny thing is, it's really not that difficult. We don't think like a man! Ladies, can we talk?

Think Like a Man. Oh yes girl, I saw the movie and agree with many aspects of it. But one thing men don't understand is a woman's greatest weapon is her MIND! We are masterminds! We can do some crazy things. I know I have. I can tell you some crazy stories because in my lifetime I've had some crazy friends (and you know you have, too). You know we have been a weapon of mass distraction for a long time. I have had friends who have made me pretend to be other people on the phone to find out where their "man" was (I have played this role a couple of times). Some have checked their boyfriend or husband's cell phone while others have called jobs, friends, family maybe not realizing that *"hurt comes with dirt."* (Just thought of this phrase today). We can spice up anything, entice anyone (if we want). We play mind games and then wonder why men fire back at us. Is it simply because we are a "weapon of mass distraction"?

II

Let's analyze this word "weapon." Merriam-Webster's dictionary says that a "weapon" can be used to injure, defeat, or destroy. Well ladies, you know there have been times when we have wanted to "injure" someone because they hurt our feelings. And, being human, we wanted to get back at them. We knew this wasn't right, but at the time it sure felt good. I don't know anyone who enjoys being hurt especially by someone they love. At times, some of us, even go for the gusto, and want to destroy that person—and that's not right either. Look at the word "defeat." We use "weapons" because not only do we want to defeat the other person, but we also don't want to be defeated. Well, put your weapons down, ladies. Yes, that's what I said. Stop slinging the guns of jealousy, envy, hatred, and anger towards women, and especially towards men. Put your emotional guns back in the holster and use one of the greatest weapons God ever gave you—YOUR MIND!

III

When I was growing up so many of my friends and acquaintances would fight over boys. Yeah, they used to throw down over one young boy and the crazy thing about it is, even if they won—THEY DIDN'T GET THE GUY! He would either keep the other girl or decide he didn't want either one of them. But there they were with their guns of anger drawn in the air.

Now that I am older and have experienced many things, I realize that it's time for us to become a different kind of "distraction." Why don't we women "distract" other women from petty competiveness by letting them know we are all in this together and although we have different types of struggles, one sistah is no better than the other? We all cry, hurt, bleed, and feel pain. Let's raise each other up instead of constantly tearing each other down. It's really wonderful to see a woman excel in her career, buy a new house, continue her education or even try something new, but what is mind-boggling is why so many other women become what young people call "haters." Guess what, even if that woman flaunts everything she has (which is wrong on her part), keep your guns in the sling because each of us have to answer to God for what we do. Find ways to celebrate her, to lift her up. Remember, your turn is coming, too.

IV

Why don't we encourage those men in our lives, men who may not have enough ambition or drive, why don't we encourage them to get a college education, or a decent-paying job? Let's sow positive dream seeds in their lives so they will shoot for the stars. Why don't we persuade them to save money? Why do we women always take from them? Perhaps every now and then we could pay for a meal, gas, or a movie. Everyone loves to be treated—even the men in our lives, in our families or in our circle of friends. Why don't we invite these men to church? Even if they say, "No," at least we extended an invitation. Why don't we let both men and women know that with Christ we have everything? Why don't we share the gospel and let others know that they are "more than conquerors" if they have Jesus Christ in their life?

Oh yes, ladies! We *are* weapons of mass distraction, but we have a new mission. We must distract men and women for the greater, the better, the higher, the more promising, realizing that God has given us this ability to win souls for him! So examine your new "weapons" —the Word of God, that beautiful smile, that tender, giving heart, that sweet disposition, that supportive nature, that Child-of-God walk and talk—and celebrate because God has made you a new creature in Christ. Let's use our weapons to distract men and women away from the wicked ways of the world towards the blessings that can only be found in the Kingdom of God.

Here's to Old School

Remember the former things of old...
Isaiah 46:9, KJV

Here's to Old School...
Vaseline-shined shoes, platforms with
Taps on the bottoms and oh those Penny Loafers!
The mini skirt brought it up,
The maxi brought it down,
The bell bottoms brought it wide
And we thought we were stylin' in
Our Lee Jeans.
But you were nobody, nobody unless you wore
Puma, Converse or Pro-Keds,
And if you didn't have them on
They would just look at you and say,
"You got on Skips."

Here's to Old School...
Aluminum foil on the end of our antennas. What?
We had a clear picture before there was cable
Could watch *Gigantor* and *Go Speed Racer* with
No problem.

Or we would just listen to our 45's or LP's inside
Or sit on the steps with our Boom Box outside
Rockin' our Afro puffs with our steel afro picks.
While men profiled their Caesar haircuts and their
Jheri curls,
Women were sitting in the beauty parlors waiting
for that hot straightening comb
To sizzle through their somewhat wet scalp like
bacon in a frying pan.

Here's to Old School…
Parents cooked meals instead of ordering.
Families sat down and ate together
But on the weekends it was Chicken Delight
Or some Swanson TV dinner or Chicken Pot Pie.
And in the evening when we wanted to relax
we remembered that
Chock Full of Nuts was still a Heavenly Coffee
And Charlie still said he "loves his Good 'N Plenty."

Here's to Old School…
Calling our friends on the Walkie Talkie
Or on our cheap CB Radio.
Trying to get the Korectotype to work on our

Swing-the-carriage typewriters.
Then so frustrated, steppin' outside to play
Mother, May I? or Red Light, Green Light 1-2-3,
Stickball, punch ball, basketball
Or just plain old marbles, Jacks,
Double Dutch or Hopscotch,
While climbing trees, playing Celo,
Or Spin the Bottle.
We went from Shoe Shine to Moon Shine.

Here's to Old School...
New school, we know you play by different rules,
But respect is universal.
God is the same yesterday, today, and forever.
He kept us and he'll keep you.
What we did may have been crazy
And unconventional
And just plain out of the ordinary,
But we wouldn't change a thing because
It made us who we are today.
So, here's to Old School!

The Yard

Whatever happens, keep thanking God...
This is what God wants you to do.
1 Thessalonians 5:18

The smell of tantalizing barbecue smoke rising from the grill and the sound of fried fish sizzling greet you as you walk up the stone-paved driveway. The silky, green grass and the one huge tree that provides shade on a sunny day, throw out the welcome mat, as well. Here is a place of quiet rest, yet unspeakable joy. This is a place that brings together family and friends through music, food, and fun. The surroundings are simple—a garage that needed to be fixed-up when we first moved in, a driveway that needed to be paved, as well as some grassy areas and plants that needed to be cultivated and cared for. The location of our house was ideal—not too far from the grocery stores and schools, not too far from our church, and it was easy to reach from the highway. Although many people came to visit us and sit for a spell inside the house, countless others travelled for miles in the spring and summer months to come to what we call, "The Yard."

Rewind a little more than 40 years ago when two young women from Alabama decided they wanted a place of their own. (I was a teenager when my mother and my aunt bought the house). When the two sisters pooled their resources, little did they know that their white house, with the yard, would make a profound impact on the lives of those who lived there or those who came to visit.

"The Yard" became quite popular as the years went by, and it blessed those who came to fellowship with us. It was so popular that our family began to use a large calendar for scheduling purposes in order not to double-book events! These events trigger many memories, but a few everyday ones stand out in my mind. I remember a tricycle that my uncle, who is now deceased, brought home from his job. Every young person in our family rode that bike. We never got rid of it. We kept it in memory of my uncle and the times spent with him in "The Yard." I remember him teaching me how to barbecue using a real charcoal grill. And, I recall him showing me how to keep the tomato plants standing tall by using a stick. He cautioned me, while noshing steadily on his peanuts, to avoid accidents by not only looking at the brake lights of a car, but also by paying attention to the driver's back wheels. He introduced me to the southern phrase, "none-na." "What does that mean?" I asked. He laughed heartily. "Stay out of grown folks' business because it is 'none-na' (none of) your business."

"The Yard" is a haven for many. Even the seniors of our church sometimes come just to relax. This simple place hosts everybody's birthday party (and there are a lot of us). My daughter's engagement, wedding, and the blessing of her second child were all held there. But we didn't need a party to take our place at the table in "The Yard." One would think it was all about the barbecue, but it wasn't. There was something about the Spirit of God being around, and, among us that made the time special. We would cook Sunday dinners to eat outside on nice days. On other days, the desserts that my aunt and cousin made would reign supreme, or we would just sit there and eat ice cream and "chill." When we planned our Family Reunion Fish Fry, I didn't think everyone would fit, but "The Yard" opened its arms and embraced us all.

My family thrived on games. Games, games, and more games. Some of us were fiercely competitive, others not so much. But we all wanted to have fun and win, if we could. We played Spades, Dominoes, Scrabble (on the board back then), Monopoly, Checkers, and my favorite, Bid Whist. Years ago, we even had a basketball hoop for the athletic and the wannabe NBA players. Lately, we have resorted to games such as "Red Light, Green Light 123" with my younger grandson, and playing volleyball and listening to music with my older grandson. When we weren't playing games, it was just good to entertain family and friends from our home state and those from states across the country.

Everyone who journeyed to the back of our white house knew they would be changed. "The Yard" would brighten someone's day, relax someone's mind, and put a smile on someone's face. There was a deep sense of excitement when friends knew they were coming to a barbeque or an event. I began to realize that some, even in the midst of their trouble or pain, would look forward to having their hearts lifted when they came to "The Yard."

As I reflect on the impact "The Yard" has had on friends and family, I am reminded that we ought not to take the simple things in life for granted. Sometimes we look at what we don't have, when we need to thank God for all he has generously provided. We may never know just how God is going to use us or the blessings he has given us for His glory..

Nowadays when I walk outside, I often see my older aunts and my mother (all in their 70's and 80's) sitting in the garage that's part of "The Yard," talking about old times or hard times, laughing, and having fun with the kids and other family members. I smile as I wonder aloud what draws them together. After all, this yard is not as large as others on our block. It doesn't even have a swimming pool or a deck. But what it does have is the outpouring of God's Spirit into the heart of two sisters who graciously extend hospitality to others. Today, more than 40 years later, I know I am truly grateful to God for what we call, "The Yard."

It Has or Will Happen to you, Boo!

Gray hair is a glorious crown worn by those who have lived right. Proverbs 16:31

I need to buy me a "forget-me-not" plant.
Yeah, that sounds a little crazy
But I try to put things in a real safe place
Then it's safe from me—now that's hazy!
I just had it in my hand and put it down over there.
I just need to take my time.
Sometimes I find it and sometimes I don't.
Am I going out of my mind?
IT HAS OR WILL HAPPEN TO YOU, BOO!

I walk in a room for something I need
And I stand in the middle of the floor.
I rack my brain over and over again.
And say, "What did I come in here for?
Then I search all over the place looking for my glasses,
I even look under the bed.
And the painful thing that I soon find out

Is that the glasses are on top of my head!
IT HAS OR WILL HAPPEN TO YOU, BOO!

Sometimes I see a person in a store
And we stand awhile and chat
And they say, "I know you remember my name."
And I say, "Now, you know better than that."
We linger and talk about good times
And they break down some serious facts.
Then they leave and turn the corner
And I say, "Who in the world was that?"
IT HAS OR WILL HAPPEN TO YOU, BOO!

Now what happens when you're really thirsty
While carrying around your speakerphone,
You put the phone in the refrigerator
And continue to carry on the conversation alone.
Then you sit down to watch some TV
And you want to flip to another station,
You're pressing buttons left and right
Just about to lose your patience.
It seems that the device you found isn't working
But let the truth be told...
You were using the telephone to turn the channels

And not the remote control.
IT HAS OR WILL HAPPEN TO YOU, BOO!

And then that dreaded little mobile device
It sometimes can be the pits.
When you ask someone, "Can you call my phone?"
And still can't find it.
Now you go and look in the car
To see if the phone is there
You fish around in your bag
And say, "It's got to be here somewhere."
You find your phone and lose your keys.
Every day seems to throw you a curve
But it's just one of those days of hide and seek,
But my goodness, it gets on your nerves.
IT HAS OR WILL HAPPEN TO YOU, BOO!

Even when our "forgetter" fails to remember,
And our "remember" fails to forget,
We should live life to the fullest
And never have any regrets.
Because our "remember" mechanism
May not work all the days of our lives,
And that "forgetter" mind we have
Always seems to want to drive.

But when you are truly grateful
To the Lord for filling your cup,
Quit worrying when your mind feels empty,
Just thank God for waking you up.

LIVING ON GOD'S GRACE

My grace is sufficient...
2 Corinthians 12:9, KJV

When I wake up in the morning
(Not in despair)
Knowing someone cares,
Realizing that God is always there,
I'm not just living on God's goodness,
I'm living on His grace.

With or without a decent paying job,
If I'm healthy and strong,
Feeling like I belong
Can rise above problems when people
treat me wrong,
I'm not only living on God's mercy,
I'm just living on His grace.

When life seems like more than I can bear
He makes my heavy burdens light.
Let's me know I'll be alright
Because I'm precious in His sight.

I'm not only living on God's faithfulness,
I'm just living on His grace.

When I think about the amazing grace
That He has showered on me,
His love can never be replaced
His only Son took my place...
He filled that empty space.
I'm not just living on God's loving-kindness,
I'm living on His Grace.

And when your steps grow tired,
Remember to take a Sabbath rest.
Praise God for what you have accomplished,
And for helping you pass each test.

As you reflect on just how far you've come
While you run this challenging race,
Understand that you are now and have always been
Living on God's amazing grace.

CPSIA information can be obtained
at www.ICGtesting.com
Printed in the USA
LVHW081155260121
677516LV00006B/423